LIFE IN AN OLD GROWTH FOREST

LIFE IN AN OLD GROWTH FOREST

BY VALERIE RAPP
PHOTOGRAPHS BY FRANK STAUB

Lerner Publications Company
Minneapolis

To Sarah, Leah, and Adam Skrine. Live your dreams and be strong. Your dreams can come true. Love, Val

Lerner Publications Company
A division of Lerner Publishing Group
241 First Avenue North
Minneapolis, MN 55401 U.S.A.

Website address: www.lernerbooks.com

Library of Congress Cataloging-in-Publication Data

Rapp, Valerie.
    Life in an old growth forest / by Valerie Rapp ; photos by Frank Staub.
        p.   cm. — (Ecosystems in action)
    Summary: Describes the ecosystem of the Douglas fir, the old growth forests of the Pacific Northwest, the effects of human activities on them, and efforts to protect them.
    ISBN: 0-8225-2135-0 (lib. bdg. : alk. paper)
    1. Old growth forest ecology—Northwest, Pacific—Juvenile literature. 2. Douglas fir—Ecology—Northwest, Pacific—Juvenile literature. [1. Douglas fir. 2. Old growth forests. 3. Forest ecology. 4. Ecology.] I. Staub, Frank J., ill. II. Title. III. Series.
QH104.5.N6 R35 2003
577.3'09795—dc21   2002003299

Manufactured in the United States of America
1 2 3 4 5 6 – JR – 08 07 06 05 04 03

CONTENTS

INTRODUCTION
WHAT IS AN ECOSYSTEM?

Human beings are not alone in this world. We live with an incredible variety of living things. There are animals of all shapes, sizes, and kinds, like tigers, rattlesnakes, and mosquitoes. Plants come in all shapes and sizes too, like pine trees, cacti, and grasses.

Plants and animals live in almost every part of the world, in all their incredible variety. But they are not distributed randomly. You never see a polar bear in the jungle, or a cactus in a swamp. Each kind of plant or animal is adapted to live in a certain kind of environment.

Each type of environment has a group of plant and animal species that are adapted to that environment. This group of plants, animals, and other organisms, along with the climate, soil, water, and air of the place where they live, is called an ecosystem. The earth has many kinds of ecosystems. Just a few examples are desert, tropical jungle, tundra, and salt marsh.

THE THREE ELEMENTS OF AN ECOSYSTEM

All ecosystems have three main elements: composition, structures, and functions. When scientists study an ecosystem, they analyze it in terms of these three parts.

Composition is the different species of plants and animals that live in the ecosystem. The old growth forests of the Pacific Northwest have Douglas firs, western hemlocks, and other kinds of trees. Some typical animal species are spotted owls, red tree voles, and martens.

Structures are the physical parts of an ecosystem that we can see and touch. In the old growth forest, big trees are important structures.

Functions are activities and processes that go on in an ecosystem. The five basic functions are input, production, recycling, storage, and output. All of these functions must go on for the ecosystem to exist.

Input is living things, materials, or

energy brought into an ecosystem, such as a tree capturing energy through photosynthesis. Production is the "manufacturing" of resources within the ecosystem: a tree grows taller, or a flying squirrel gives birth to baby squirrels.

Resources are recycled through the ecosystem when a fallen tree decays. Resources are also stored in the ecosystem—an old growth tree "stores" wood in its trunk. Output is living things, materials, or energy leaving the ecosystem: a spotted owl migrates to another forest, or loggers remove trees.

In a healthy ecosystem, the functions are in balance. For example, recycling must be roughly in balance with production. Dead plants and animals must be recycled back into the ecosystem through rot and decay, or the forest will become choked with fallen trees and waste. If the functions become severely out of balance it may take centuries for the ecosystem to recover.

The old growth Douglas fir forest is an ecosystem found only in parts of the Pacific Northwest. This ecosystem is unique among all the world's forest ecosystems because of the size and age of the trees. Some of the giant redwoods in California are bigger than the trees in the Douglas fir forests. But the Pacific Northwest has many species of big trees, not just one. Some of the bristlecone pines in Nevada live longer

THE OLD GROWTH DOUGLAS FIR FOREST IS AN ECOSYSTEM FOUND ONLY IN PARTS OF THE PACIFIC NORTHWEST. THIS ECOSYSTEM IS UNIQUE AMONG ALL THE WORLD'S FOREST ECOSYSTEMS BECAUSE OF THE SIZE AND AGE OF THE TREES.

But the Pacific Northwest has many species of trees that live a very long time. No other forest in the world that has a group of tree species can match the trees in the Douglas fir old growth forest for their huge size and long lives.

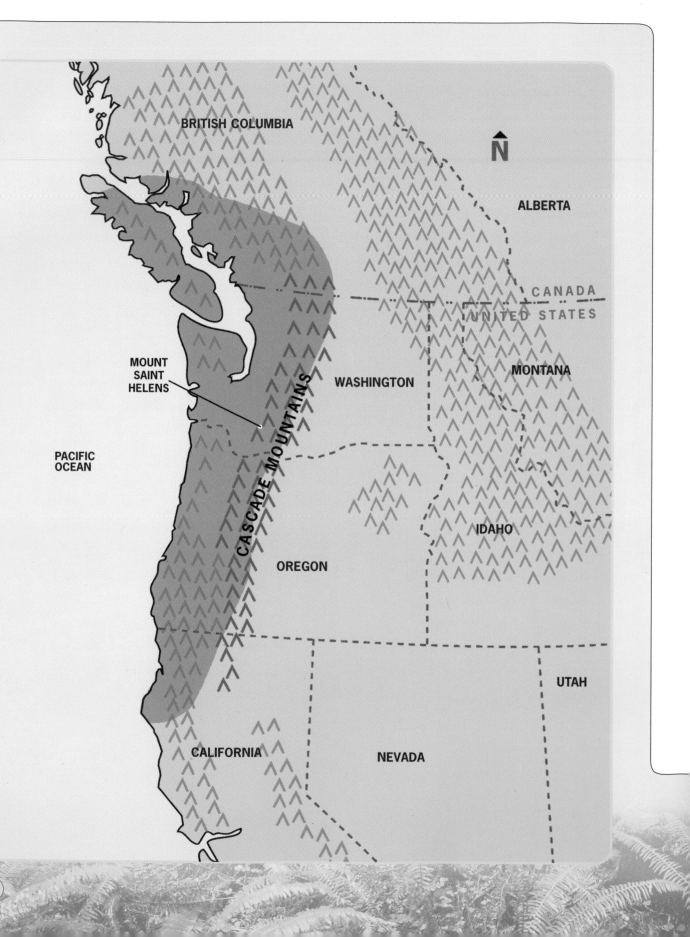

BRITISH COLUMBIA

N

ALBERTA

CANADA
UNITED STATES

MONTANA

WASHINGTON

MOUNT
SAINT
HELENS

CASCADE MOUNTAINS

PACIFIC
OCEAN

IDAHO

OREGON

UTAH

CALIFORNIA

NEVADA

CHAPTER 1

A UNIQUE FOREST ECOSYSTEM

Each different type of forest, including the old growth forest of the Pacific Northwest, has a unique combination of tree species. Although there are hundreds of tree species, they all fall into two main types: hardwoods and conifers.

Hardwood trees have leaves, like the familiar maple and oak trees. Many hardwood trees are deciduous—they lose their leaves in the fall, and grow new leaves each spring. Some hardwoods, such as holly and live oak, are evergreens—they keep their leaves all winter. Hardwoods have flowers, like apple blossoms, and then produce seeds. The seeds may be enclosed in a fruit, like an apple, or in a nut, like an acorn. The forests in the northeastern United States are made up primarily of deciduous hardwood trees, like maple, oak, beech, and hickory.

Conifer trees have needles instead of leaves, and they produce their seeds in cones. Most conifers are evergreen—they keep their needles year-round. They shed a few old needles each year and grow some new ones, but keep most of their needles through the winter. Some common conifers are pines, firs, spruces, hemlocks, and cedars.

MIST IN AN OLD GROWTH FOREST IN WASHINGTON STATE'S MOUNT RAINIER NATIONAL PARK

Most forests in the western United States are coniferous forests, where most of the trees are conifers. The western climate varies a great deal, with many extremes of cold, heat, and drought. While hardwood trees can tolerate cold winters, they generally need warm, humid summers such as those found in the eastern United States. Conifers can survive the dry summers that are common in the western United States.

Not all coniferous forests are the same. In the western United States, differences in climate and geography help to create different kinds of coniferous forests. In the Rocky Mountains, for example, pine trees are the dominant conifers. A dominant plant or animal is the most common plant or animal in a particular ecosystem. Or, it can be the plant or animal that has the most

influence on the ecosystem. High up in the mountains, where winters are very cold and long, true firs may be the dominant trees. On the plains below the Rocky Mountains, the climate may be too dry for any trees to grow, so the ecosystem may be a grassland or a desert. In western Oregon and Washington, which are part of the Pacific Northwest, Douglas firs are the dominant conifers.

A FOREST BECOMES OLD GROWTH WHEN IT DEVELOPS FOR HUNDREDS OF YEARS WITHOUT ANY MAJOR DISTURBANCE, SUCH AS A FOREST FIRE OR LOGGING.

OLD GROWTH FORESTS OF THE PACIFIC NORTHWEST

A forest becomes old growth when it develops for hundreds of years without any major disturbance, such as a forest fire or logging. When a forest grows a long time with only small disturbances, it develops into a very different ecosystem from a young forest.

The old growth forests of the Pacific Northwest are found in an area stretching from southwestern British Columbia to northern California. The area extends from the ocean inland to the crest of the Cascade Mountains. Although all of this area has the potential to grow old growth forests, this type of forest actually covers only part of the area. The old growth forests are scattered over the Pacific Northwest, usually in between areas of younger forests.

The unique climate in this area shapes this ecosystem. The Pacific Northwest has mild, wet winters and warm, dry summers. Although hardwood trees could survive the mild winters, most hardwoods cannot take the dry summers. So the old growth forest is a coniferous forest. The winters are very wet, with lots of rain and snow. As a result, Douglas firs, western hemlocks, western red cedars, and true firs are the dominant tree species. The east side of the Cascades is much drier, with colder winters, so pine forests grow there.

A Douglas fir forest in the Pacific Northwest is at least two hundred years old before it develops old growth

DOUGLAS FIR
(*PSEUDOTSUGA MENZIESII*)

characteristics. To be an old growth forest today, it must have been undisturbed by major changes since at least the late 1700s, not long after George Washington was president. An old growth forest can be anywhere from two hundred to one thousand years old. A thousand-year-old forest would have started growing when it was still the Middle Ages in Europe.

When you walk in an old growth forest, you feel like you are walking in a giant cathedral. The world outside the forest seems like it is far, far away. You hear the wind in the treetops, but it is high above you. It might be a very hot day, but in the forest it is cool. You are protected by the huge, old trees. When you look up, you see the treetops as high above you as a fifteen-story building. You can see patches of sky only in a few gaps between the thick tree branches. The sunlight is filtered through the tree canopy like light coming through a stained glass window made of many shades of green. You are walking on a thick layer of soft, emerald green moss. You might touch the rough, gray bark of a Douglas fir. The tree is so big that three people stretching out their arms and joining hands could not make a circle all the way around it.

COMPOSITION OF THE OLD GROWTH FOREST

Everywhere you look in the old growth forest, you see layer on layer of living things. Shrubs and young hemlock trees grow from old decaying logs on the ground. Even the trees have other plants growing on them—moss drapes the lower branches, and sometimes ferns grow out of the moss. You probably won't see them, but flying squirrels nest in the high branches, and woodpeckers feed on the insects found in the standing dead trees. Eventually, the dead trees will fall to the ground and the seeds of new trees will sprout in the rotten wood.

The complexity of the old growth forest—the many layers of living things—is an important part of what makes the old growth forest special. Scientists who study forests have found that an old growth forest has many more different species of plants and animals than a younger forest.

For instance, an old growth forest has more kinds of spiders and more kinds of insects than a younger forest. Scientists use the word *biodiversity* to describe this quality. *Biodiversity* comes from *bio*, meaning "life," and *diversity*, meaning "variety." Forests that are less than two hundred years old usually do not have as much biodiversity as older forests.

STRUCTURE OF AN OLD GROWTH FOREST

Why are old growth forests so rich in biodiversity? Scientists have found that four key structural features make the old growth forest different from younger forests. The forest structures create habitats—places where plants or animals normally live and grow—for the different species that are found only in old growth forests. The structures also have a lot to do with the unique ways that energy and nutrients are cycled through an old growth forest. Understanding the structures, therefore, is basic to understanding the old growth forest. The four structural features of an old growth forest are large, old growth trees; a

(ABOVE) **FLYING SQUIRREL**
(*GLAUCOMYS SABRINUS*)

(RIGHT) **MOSSES AND OTHER PLANTS GROW ON FALLEN TREES IN AN OLD GROWTH FOREST.**

multilayered canopy; snags; and large, fallen trees on land and in streams.

The canopy is the horizontal top layer of the forest formed by the tree branches. The old growth trees have many large branches, and trees of different ages, sizes, and heights grow beneath the tallest trees. All the trees' branches together create a deep, multilayered canopy with a variety of habitats for plants and animals. Because of this multilayered canopy, the old growth forest has a different climate at the treetops than it does on the forest floor.

Snags are large, dead trees that are still standing. Snags provide essential habitat for many animals, from insects to spotted owls. These standing dead trees are also a storehouse of nutrients for the ecosystem.

Eventually all trees fall, whether live or dead. An old growth forest has lots of logs lying on the forest floor, in various stages of decay. These rotting logs provide nutrients to the ecosystem, and they contribute to the functions of the ecosystem. Fallen logs also provide habitat for many small animals.

(ABOVE) **FUNGI AND MOSSES GROW ON FALLEN LOGS.**

(LEFT) **THE OLD GROWTH FOREST HAS A WIDE VARIETY OF PLANT SPECIES, INCLUDING SOME HARDWOOD TREES.**

FUNCTIONS OF AN OLD GROWTH FOREST

The five basic functions of an ecosystem are input, production, recycling, storage, and output. Each plant and animal carries out most or all of the functions during its lifetime. A western hemlock tree may start life on top of a rotting tree, and help to recycle that tree. As the young hemlock grows, it brings energy into the forest through photosynthesis. The tree grows larger, and its trunk eventually becomes a massive storehouse of nutrients. Finally, the nutrients in its wood become available to the ecosystem again after the hemlock dies. During its life, the hemlock also provides a home to insects, birds, and other animals.

Each function is carried out by many different species. Bark beetles, ambrosia beetles, carpenter ants, termites, many kinds of fungi, and eventually ferns and young trees all help to recycle a fallen tree. Each beetle or carpenter ant takes only a small bite. Each fungus digests only a little bit. Yet over the centuries, millions of small bites and little bits can recycle an entire giant tree.

WESTERN HEMLOCK (*TSUGA HETEROPHYLLA*) GROWING ON A FALLEN TREE

CHAPTER 2
THE BIG TREES:
KEY TO THE OLD GROWTH FOREST

How big are the trees in the old growth forest? The biggest known Douglas fir is 280 feet (85 meters) tall, and 13.5 feet (4.11 meters) in diameter. The tree trunk alone weighs about 175 tons (160 metric tons). In comparison, the blue whale, which is the largest animal on earth, weighs up to 150 tons (140 metric tons). So the champion Douglas fir is much heavier than a blue whale.

Not every old growth tree is a champion, of course. But even the smaller old growth trees are big. An old growth tree is commonly 200 feet (60 meters) or more tall, unless the top has broken off in a storm. In comparison, the Statue of Liberty is 305 feet (93.0 meters) tall from the ground to the top of the torch. So the average old growth tree is two-thirds as tall as the Statue of Liberty. The biggest known Douglas fir is actually just 25 feet (7.6

meters) shorter than the Statue of Liberty.

An old growth tree's trunk is big in diameter, too. It can be anywhere from 3 feet (1 meter) to 20 feet (6 meters) thick. Measure out 20 feet and imagine a tree that big around.

Everything is impressive about these big trees. Scientists have estimated that a single old growth tree can have over sixty million individual needles. These giant trees also have extensive root systems. Some of the bigger roots may be as much as 1 foot (30 centimeters) in diameter—bigger than the trunks of some small trees.

One reason why old growth trees get so big is because they live long lives. An old growth tree can live from five hundred to one thousand years. A tree that is five hundred years old today sprouted into a seedling about the time that Columbus first landed on an island in the Bahamas.

A thousand-year-old tree started life while the Vikings were still attacking England.

A tree does not feel or see the things that happen to it in the same way that we do, but it is changed by the events in its long life. Along with beautiful summer days and sunshine, an old growth tree lives through cold winter rains, snowstorms, windstorms, summer droughts, and forest fires.

An old growth tree can often survive a forest fire. The bark may be black and charred on the outside, but it is very thick and protects the tree's inner wood. The tree may lose some branches and be scarred by the fire, but it survives.

Windstorms break off branches and sometimes snap off the whole top of a tree. When that happens, the uppermost side branch starts to grow straight up and creates a new tree trunk. This new trunk, however, comes from the side of the tree. If a tree falls in a windstorm, it may scrape against another tree, breaking off branches and leaving scars where it scraped the bark.

Each old growth tree develops its own highly individual character, through all the events of its long life. Its crown, or top, takes on a unique shape. It may have two

(ABOVE) **A TREE SCARRED BY A FOREST FIRE**
(LEFT) **OLD GROWTH TREES HAVE EXTENSIVE ROOT SYSTEMS.**

or three great forked branches at the top, each branch as big as a small tree. It may have a broken top or a forked trunk. The tree may lean to one side, or it may have twisted or bent branches. There may be many gaps along the trunk where branches are missing. When it is looked at from the side, the tree may look like a tall bottlebrush with many of its bristles missing, because branches have broken off.

By the time a tree gets to be hundreds of years old, it is scarred and tough. If trees could talk, each old growth tree would have its own story to tell. And what amazing stories they would be, as each tree told its story of hundreds of years of life in the forest.

The big trees have many important functions in the forest. An old growth tree is both a factory and a storehouse for the forest. It is a factory because it produces the food base for the rest of the system, through photosynthesis. Like all green plant leaves, the tree's green needles change sunlight to chemical energy. Through this process, the needles provide the simple sugars and carbohydrates that the tree needs to grow.

An old growth tree is also a storehouse, because its wood is an enormous accumulation of biomass. Biomass is the total weight of all living plants and animals in a given area. The old growth tree takes much of the energy it gets from photosynthesis and turns it into wood. As the tree grows larger, the amount of wood becomes enormous. This wood is a storehouse of organic materials and nutrients. After the tree dies, its wood will be used for hundreds of years by many plants and animals.

> LIKE ALL GREEN PLANT LEAVES, THE TREE'S GREEN NEEDLES CHANGE SUNLIGHT TO CHEMICAL ENERGY. THROUGH THIS PROCESS, THE NEEDLES PROVIDE THE SIMPLE SUGARS AND CARBOHYDRATES THAT THE TREE NEEDS TO GROW.

SNAGS

Eventually, even a long-lived old growth tree dies. A tree may be killed by lightning, burned in a severe forest fire, blown over in a windstorm, or knocked over in a landslide. It may be killed by heavy insect damage from Douglas fir bark beetles or other insects, or it may die from one of many tree diseases. Most tree diseases, such as heart rot and root rot, are caused by fungi or bacteria. Heart rot attacks the heartwood in the center of the tree, while root rot attacks the tree's root system. Tree diseases can spread from an infected tree to another tree, just as you might catch a cold from someone who is already sick.

But in a sense, an old growth tree goes on living after it dies. Dead trees provide two of the other key structures in the old growth forest ecosystem: snags and fallen trees. An old growth tree continues to play an important part in the ecosystem for hundreds of years after it dies.

Snags, or standing dead trees, have several important roles. A snag can continue to stand in the forest for fifty to two hundred years after the tree dies.

(TOP) **DEAD TREES THAT REMAIN STANDING ARE CALLED SNAGS.** (RIGHT) **SOME TREES ARE KILLED BY A DISEASE CALLED HEART ROT.**

THE BIG TREES OF THE OLD GROWTH FOREST

Douglas Fir *(Pseudotsuga menziesii)*
Height: 230–260 feet (70–80 meters)
Trunk diameter: 5–7 feet (150–200 centimeters)
Life span: five hundred to one thousand years

The champion big tree is in Olympic National Park in Washington. It is approximately 280 feet (85 meters) tall and its trunk is 13.5 feet (4.11 meters) in diameter. The Douglas fir has single needles 0.75–1.25 inches (2–3 centimeters) long that are flat and rounded at the tip. Cones are 2–3.5 inches (5–9 centimeters) long, with three-pointed bracts (scalelike leaves) that look like the hind legs and tail of a mouse protruding from between the scales. Large trees have very thick bark with deep furrows and rough

texture. The wood is light colored, straight grained, and strong. The Douglas fir is the most valuable lumber tree in the Pacific Northwest; the wood is used for lumber, plywood, and many wood products. The thick bark of an old growth Douglas fir protects it from fire. These big trees can often survive a forest fire, even though their bark may be blackened and charred.

Western Hemlock *(Tsuga heterophylla)*

Height: 160–210 feet (50–65 meters)

Trunk diameter: 3–4 feet (90–120 centimeters)

Life span: four hundred to five hundred years

The champion big tree is in Olympic National Forest in Washington. It is over 190 feet (58 meters) tall, and its trunk is 9 feet (3 meters) in diameter. The western hemlock has single needles 0.25–0.75 inch (0.6–2 centimeters) long that are arranged in two flat rows along each branch. Cones are small, 0.75–1 inch (2–2.5 centimeters) long, and tan, and they hang down at the ends of branches. The bark is furrowed, but not as deeply as Douglas fir bark. The wood is not as valuable as that of the Douglas fir, but it is used for lumber and pulp for paper, and is a source of cellulose used to make rayon and cellophane. The leader, or growing top, of the tree always droops over. Western hemlock grows well in shade, and seedlings often grow on rotting logs on the forest floor.

Western Red Cedar *(Thuja plicata)*

Height: more than 200 feet (60 meters)

Trunk diameter: 5–10 feet (150–300 centimeters)

Life span: over one thousand years

The champion tree is in Olympic National Park in Washington. Although it is only

160 feet (49 meters) tall, its trunk is 20 feet (6 meters) in diameter. Western red cedars have scalelike needles 0.06–0.13 inch (less than 0.5 centimeter) long; the needles make fernlike sprays that hang from the main branches. Cones are about 0.5 inch (1.3 centimeters) long and leather brown, and sit upright on foliage. Bark is reddish brown, thin, and stringy. The wood is reddish brown, very resistant to rot, straight grained, and fragrant. It is very valuable for making roofing shakes, siding, fence posts, and cedar chests. It was the most valuable tree for the Indians, who used planks to build houses, logs for canoes, bark for clothing, and roots for baskets. Western red cedar likes wet soils, and often forms cedar groves near streams. The trees are often fluted at the base and taper rapidly from their thick buttresses near the ground.

Pacific Silver Fir *(Abies amabilis)*

Height: 150–180 feet (45–55 meters)

Trunk diameter: 3–4 feet (90–120 centimeters)

Life span: more than four hundred years

The champion big tree is near Forks, Washington. It is approximately 200 feet (60 meters) tall,

with a trunk 8 feet (over 2 meters) in diameter. Pacific silver fir has single needles 0.75–1.5 inches (2–4 centimeters) long that curve upward in two rows along branches. The needles are dark green above and silvery white on the underside. Cones are 3–6 inches (8–15 centimeters) long, barrel shaped, and green to purple, and sit upright on upper branches. Bark is light gray, smooth, and thin. The bark of younger trees may have resin-filled "blisters." The wood is weak and decays rapidly. It is used for lumber and for wood pulp. Pacific silver fir grows at middle elevations in the mountains. Squirrels often cut cones from the branches and eat the seeds. Sometimes they stash the cones and retrieve them in the winter, when other seeds are scarce.

Sitka Spruce *(Picea sitchensis)*
Height: 230–250 feet (70–75 meters)
Trunk diameter: 6–8 feet (180–240 centimeters)
Life span: more than eight hundred years

The champion big tree is in Olympic National Park, Washington. Although it is only 190 feet (58 meters) tall, its trunk is 19 feet (5.8 meters) in diameter. Sitka spruce has stiff, prickly, single needles 0.63–1 inch (1.6–2 centimeters) long that are on all sides of the branches. Cones are 2–3.5 inches (5–9 centimeters) long and light brown, and hang at the ends of branches. Bark is thin, with large, loose scales, and is often purplish brown. The wood is light but strong, and was used to build airplanes through World War II. It is now used for lumber, shelving, ladders, and racing shells. The wood is resonant, so it is used to make musical instruments like pianos and guitars. Sitka spruce grows only within a few miles of the Pacific Northwest coast, where annual rainfall is high, summers are cool with lots of fog, and winters are mild.

The old growth forest has many different sizes of snags, in various stages of decay.

Soon after a tree dies, its needles and small branches fall to the ground. Much of its bark stays in place. A great deal of activity takes place on the new snag. Bark beetles and wood-boring beetles begin to tunnel through the bark. Spiders, ants, and beetles travel on the bark's surface.

Birds like brown creepers and nuthatches patrol the bark, catching and eating insects on the bark's surface. Red-breasted sapsuckers drill small holes in horizontal lines around the tree trunk and eat the insects they find. Hairy woodpeckers also drill into the new snag, looking for insect larvae. The drilling of the woodpeckers makes a loud tat-tat-tat sound that carries a long way in the quiet forest. Pileated woodpeckers are the largest woodpeckers in North America. A pileated woodpecker is as large as a crow and has a bright red crest on top of its head. These woodpeckers chisel out large, rectangular-shaped holes in their search for their favorite food, carpenter ants.

After several years, the bark begins to

(TOP) **PILEATED WOODPECKER** *(DRYOCOPUS PILEATUS)*
(BOTTOM) **BIG BROWN BAT** *(EPTESICUS FUSCUS)*

fall off the snag. Insects tunnel deeper into the wood. Fungi get into the wood through the insect tunnels, and the snag's wood begins to decay and soften. If the tree died of heart rot, much of the wood may be half-rotten already.

Now that the wood is softer, animals begin to dig out holes to nest in. A hole in a snag or a live tree is called a cavity, and animals that make their homes in these holes are called cavity-nesting animals. Because they are insulated by the surrounding wood, cavities stay warm in winter and cool in summer. They also stay dry and are difficult for predators to reach, making them excellent homes. Smaller birds like chestnut-backed chickadees and small woodpeckers use small holes. They may start with a natural hole and dig out wood until they get it just the way they want it. Some birds may line the bottom of the hole with moss to make a soft nest.

Eventually, larger birds and some mammals take over the holes, digging to make them larger. The spotted owl, for example, is a cavity-nester. Since it is a large bird, only a big snag can provide a hole large enough for its nest.

Bats also need snags, although they don't nest in them. Bats use snags as day roosts. These winged mammals are nocturnal, meaning they sleep during the day and are active at night. They begin flying at dusk, using their sonar to find their way as they dart and swoop after insects. During the day, they need a shady, sheltered place to roost. Bats find loose slabs of bark on snags and creep under them. There, they sleep hanging upside down, clinging to the bark with their feet. Bats do much of their foraging outside of the forest, frequently near water, where they find lots of insects. But they need the shelter of snags in old growth forests during the day.

A snag decays more and more as the years go by. Bark sloughs off the snag, building up a mound at its base. Over the years, Douglas fir snags gradually come apart from the top down, with large chunks breaking off as the wood rots, until only a short stub is left. Western red cedar snags, on the other hand, usually lose only their bark, and stand whole until the wood

THE SPOTTED OWL (*Strix occidentalis*)

The spotted owl is about the size of a raven, or 16 to 19 inches (41–48 centimeters) long. The owl's back is dark brown, and its head and neck have round, white spots. Its wings and chest are covered with light brown and white spots. In addition to needing snags, the spotted owl depends on the multi-layered canopy to protect it from predators. It flutters and dodges among the layers of treetops to avoid such swift predators as great horned owls and goshawks.

The female spotted owl lays only two eggs in her nest, and a spotted owl pair may not nest every year. Both parent owls hunt to feed their young, and both defend their nest from predators. The owls need forests that provide plenty of prey animals. They hunt flying squirrels, red tree voles, and other small mammals. These small mammals need the various structures of the old growth forest for their own habitat, so the spotted owls often find their best hunting in old growth forests.

rots through at ground level and the whole snag falls. An old, rotten snag may have huckleberry bushes or even young trees growing on the broken top of its trunk.

A snag is a reservoir of nutrients for the forest ecosystem. While standing, it provides habitat for many animals and some plants. As it decays, it gives nutrients back to the ecosystem. When the wood at its center becomes rotten enough, the snag no longer has the strength to stand, and it topples easily on a windy day. It may seem sad to see a giant of the forest fall over.

But change is a healthy, normal part of the old growth forest. The gifts of fallen trees are vital to the forest's future.

When an old growth tree finally falls, it creaks and groans as the wood breaks. It falls slowly at first, then picks up speed. If it hits other trees on the way down, it may knock them over, too. The tree hits the ground with a loud boom that sounds like thunder. The ground shakes for hundreds of feet around the fallen tree. After a minute, all the echoes finish coming back, and the forest is quiet again.

THIS TREE FELL BETWEEN TWO STANDING TREES, BUT EVEN HERE IT SUPPORTS MOSS, LICHENS, FUNGI, AND INSECT LIFE.

CHAPTER 3

ON THE GROUND AND UNDERGROUND

When you walk in an old growth forest, it seems very quiet on the ground. But when you look more closely, you'll find that the forest floor is a rich world, full of action and biodiversity. Many of the processes that are essential to the ecosystem take place on the ground. Here, the fallen giants of the old growth forest are recycled back into the ecosystem. Underground, roots take up the water and nutrients that support the living trees. An incredible variety of plants and animals make these processes happen.

The forest floor has a deep layer of soft, emerald green moss. Large clumps of sword ferns arch gracefully above the

mossy ground. The rotting logs are covered with moss blankets. Young hemlocks and grand firs grow on top of some fallen logs. You may see mushrooms of many shapes and colors, including white or yellow coral mushrooms, orange chanterelles, and the grotesque shapes of morels.

Although the old growth forest does not have as many flowers as a meadow, it does have some flowers. In the spring, you'll see trilliums, with their three white petals, and delicate calypso orchids. In the late spring, the rhododendrons have huge, showy, pink flowers, bright against the gray-brown trunks of the trees.

Some saprophytic flowers grow on the shady forest floor. Saprophytic plants get their nourishment from decaying plants on the forest floor, so they don't need sunlight like green plants do. You might see a clump of Indian pipe, with its ghostly white stems and nodding flower that is shaped like the bowl of a smoking pipe. Candystick, which is also called sugarstick, has a red-and-white-striped stem that looks like a stick of hard candy, with small white flowers.

(OPPOSITE PAGE) **SWORD FERNS (*POLYSTICHUM MUNITUM*) COVER THE FOREST FLOOR.**
(ABOVE LEFT) **TRILLIUM (*TRILLIUM ERECTUM*)**
(ABOVE RIGHT) **CALYPSO ORCHID (*CALYPSO BULBOSA*)**

FALLEN TREES

It's not easy walking through the old growth forest, because there are fallen trees everywhere. Here, several trees fell together in last winter's windstorm. Over there lies a giant tree that fell several centuries ago. Young hemlock trees 20 feet (6 meters) tall are growing on top of the decaying log. Nearby is a gentle mound on the forest floor, covered with trees and ferns. This, too, is a fallen tree, but this tree fell five hundred years ago. It has rotted back into the ground so completely that the shape of the tree can barely be seen.

The fallen trees are an important part of the web of life in the old growth forest. As many as three hundred species of insects use fallen trees as homes during some part of their life cycle. Many kinds of mammals, birds, amphibians, and reptiles also use fallen trees for homes, food, and safe places to hide. It takes up to five hundred years for a fallen Douglas fir tree to decay on the forest floor. If a giant tree fell over in a windstorm about the same time that Columbus sighted land in 1492, it would just now be completely turned back into soil again. But all that time, while the dead tree slowly decays, it gives itself back to the living things in the forest.

The Douglas fir bark beetle is often the first insect to make the newly fallen tree its home. The bark beetle chews through the outer bark into the softer, moister, inner bark. Then the bark beetle chews tunnels through the inner bark and sapwood, feeding on the wood and laying eggs in side tunnels. Other beetles, like the

IF A GIANT TREE FELL OVER IN A WINDSTORM ABOUT THE SAME TIME THAT COLUMBUS SIGHTED LAND IN 1492, IT WOULD JUST NOW BE COMPLETELY TURNED BACK INTO SOIL AGAIN.

ambrosia beetle, also eat their way into the newly fallen tree. Redbellied checkered beetles hunt the bark beetles in their tunnels and eat them.

Other animals and plants use the insect tunnels as their way into the fallen tree. Fungus spores stick to crevices in the shells of the bark beetles, and are carried into the log's moist sapwood. There the fungi begin to grow and spread through the sapwood. The fruiting bodies of the fungi—mushrooms and bracket fungi—can be seen growing on the outside of the log.

The fallen trees absorb large quantities of water during the Pacific Northwest's wet winters. After a few years, the log is like a giant wooden sponge, full of water. During the hot, dry summers, the logs hold the moisture inside. Insects, salamanders, slugs, snails, and rodents seek out the cool, moist shelter of the fallen trees in the summer heat. They burrow in the broken bark heaped up next to the tree, dig into the soil underneath the tree, and go into the tree itself, using the tunnels first created by the bark beetles.

As the years go by, the fallen tree decays. The wood becomes softer and

MUSHROOMS ARE THE FRUITING BODIES OF FUNGI.

wetter. It looks different—it turns red, and it breaks into pieces more easily. Insects and fungi can penetrate deeper into the log, into the heartwood. Layer by layer, the tree decays and changes. As the tree becomes more rotten, a changing parade of animals and plants lives in it and on it.

Many more different kinds of animals use the fallen tree now than did when it first fell. Carpenter ants and termites chew their own tunnels deep into the heartwood. Carpenter ants eat the eggs and larvae of some insects that damage living trees, such as spruce budworm. So

the fallen tree is home to insects that help to protect the living forest.

Meanwhile, the folding-door spider spins a silken trap in old insect tunnels and pulls the tube shut around any insects that wander into its trap. Centipedes, salamanders, and shrews follow the insect tunnels into the log, preying on any animals smaller than themselves. Shrews and shrew-moles hunt centipedes, spiders, slugs, and snails.

The fallen tree is also home to many different kinds of plants. The log is covered with a soft cushion of moss. Ferns, salal, and

(ABOVE) **BANANA SLUG (*ARIOLIMAX COLUMBIANUS*)**

(NEAR RIGHT) **A FALLEN TREE THAT PROVIDES NUTRIENTS TO A YOUNG TREE IS CALLED A NURSE LOG.**

huckleberries grow on top of the log. They send roots down through the shattered outer bark into the decaying wood. Their roots follow the crevices already made by insects and fungi, and in turn create new crevices as they grow deeper into the soft wood. The plants find both moisture and nutrients in the fallen tree.

Eventually, trees take root in the log. The fallen tree is often called a nurse log at this point, because it provides a place for young trees to grow. In one hundred years, these young trees will grow tall enough to take the place that the fallen tree once occupied in the forest.

Some trees fall into streams. There, too, a fallen tree plays an important role. A pool forms on the upstream side of the log. Leaves and twigs settle to the bottom of the pool, providing food for insects. The insects, in turn, are food for fish. The fish also rest and hide in the quiet pools. A stream in an old growth forest has a "stair-step" structure, as it splashes down over the many trees that have fallen into it. During heavy rains, the logs in the streams slow the water down, hold needed soil and gravel in place, and help to prevent floods.

FALLEN TREES ARE AN IMPORTANT PART OF THE OLD GROWTH FOREST ECOSYSTEM.

Fallen trees can help a forest survive catastrophic change. During a forest fire, many small animals find a safe shelter under fallen trees. After the fire, the fallen trees offer a moist place for seeds to sprout—the seeds that will grow into the new forest.

When the volcano Mount Saint Helens erupted in 1980 in Washington, it destroyed the forest around it and covered the ground with volcanic ash. Scientists studied the land's recovery after the eruption. They found that fallen trees helped a new forest to begin growing, even through a thick layer of volcanic ash.

Year after year, the fallen tree gives itself back to the forest. Although dead, it supports a complex community of animals and plants. Eventually, the log decays completely. After four or five hundred years, the fallen tree is just a plant-covered mound on the forest floor. But the rotted wood has made the soil richer.

TRUFFLES AND VOLES

The old growth forest provides habitat for many different kinds of animals. Each species depends on the forest in certain

THESE TREES WERE KILLED IN THE VOLCANIC ERUPTION OF MOUNT SAINT HELENS BUT PROVIDED SHELTER, NUTRIENTS, AND MOISTURE THAT HELPED A NEW FOREST TO BEGIN GROWING.

ways. It may seem that while the animals and other plants need the big trees, the big trees couldn't possibly need any of the animals or other plants. When you look at the towering trees, you might think that they need nothing but sunshine, soil, and water to survive. However, quite the opposite is true. It turns out that the old growth trees, tall and strong as they are, need to form relationships with certain kinds of fungi, known as mycorrhizal fungi.

The word *mycorrhizae* means "fungus-root structures," and describes the relationships between some fungus species and plant roots. Mycorrhizal fungi grow on plants' root tips, where they form a weblike covering over the roots. The tiny threads of the fungus also grow out into the soil. As the mycorrhizal fungi surround and extend out from the roots, they act like a sponge, helping the roots to absorb water and nutrients from the soil. Most kinds of plants have mycorrhizal fungi on their roots. Trees in particular depend on mycorrhizal fungi to help their roots absorb water and nutrients. Without mycorrhizal fungi, tree seedlings may not be able to absorb

enough water to survive during the hot, dry summers of the Pacific Northwest. Sometimes the mycorrhizal fungi also protect the tree roots from root rot.

An old growth Douglas fir may have as many as three hundred different species of mycorrhizal fungi living on its roots. The fungi also depend on the tree. The fungi absorb some of the sugars and starches that the tree produces through photosynthesis. The tree sends these sugars down to the roots from the high branches, and the roots send the water and nutrients from the soil up the tall tree trunk.

Mycorrhizal fungi help trees in many ways. But when a tree seed starts to grow, the new roots need to find these important fungi in the soil. For the mycorrhizal fungi to get to the tree's roots, both roots and fungi depend on something else—the small mammals of the old growth forest.

All fungi reproduce through fruiting bodies. Some fungi produce mushrooms, which are one kind of fruiting body. Many species of mycorrhizal fungi produce another kind of fruiting body, called a truffle. These truffles are very different from chocolate truffles you may have seen in a candy shop. These truffles grow underground and look much like very small potatoes. Each truffle contains thousands of tiny spores. Spores are similar to seeds—new fungi grow from the spores.

Truffles are a favorite food of many small mammals, such as the flying squirrel and the red-backed vole. Red-backed voles tunnel along the sides of fallen logs and underneath them, and search out the truffles that they love to eat. The voles swallow thousands of tiny spores along with the truffles. They are unable to digest the spores, however, so the spores are excreted in the vole's droppings. The small pellets decay rapidly, and as they decay, the spores are released into the soil. Whenever a growing root comes into contact with a spore, the spore begins to grow into a fungus, and the fungus attaches itself to the root.

The cycle is similar with the other animals that feed on truffles. Whether it's a flying squirrel or a red-backed vole or another small rodent, the animal passes the spores through its body and the spores drop on the forest floor, eventually reaching the tree roots that need them. So the small animals of the forest floor provide a vital service to the huge trees that tower above them.

THOUSANDS OF LITTLE LEGS

An old growth forest creates many tons of organic debris—fallen trees, branches, needles, dead plants. This enormous volume of stuff must be broken down and returned to the soil so the living trees and plants can use the nutrients it contains. What happens to all the needles, leaves, and twigs that cover the ground in the forest? This stuff, which is called forest litter, is recycled by very small animals called arthropods.

Arthropods are the most numerous of all invertebrates, or animals without backbones. (Animals with backbones are called vertebrates. They include mammals, fish, reptiles, amphibians, and birds.) Insects, mites, spiders, and centipedes are all arthropods. Instead of bones, arthropods have a hard casing on the outside of their bodies, like a beetle's hard shell. They also have jointed legs and segmented bodies. The number of legs varies—insects always have six legs, spiders always have eight legs, and centipedes and millipedes have many legs. Insects, mites, spiders, and centipedes are found throughout the old growth forest, from the highest branches to the soil. But they are especially numerous in the soil.

Old growth forests have thousands of species of arthropods. In an ecosystem rich in biodiversity, arthropods are the most diverse group of animals. In a research forest in Oregon, scientists have found 143 species of vertebrates, and 3,402 species of arthropods. That's nearly twenty-five times as many arthropod species as vertebrates. And while scientists believe they have found all the vertebrate species, they think they've found only about half of the arthropod species. This great diversity shows that the arthropods as a group are playing a very important role in the ecosystem—recycling dead plant material.

Larger arthropods, such as millipedes, grind up this material first. The most common species of millipede in the old growth forest, the yellow-spotted millipede, is black with yellow spots on each segment of its body. Larger arthropods are able to digest only a little bit of the plant material, however, and much of what they eat comes out their other end, only in smaller pieces. These smaller bits are then eaten by smaller arthropods. They also digest only

YELLOW-SPOTTED MILLIPEDE (HARPAPHE HAYDENIANA)

MITES

Mites are one of the most common groups of soil arthropods in the old growth forest. Mites are arachnids, or arthropods with eight legs. Other arachnids include spiders, scorpions, and ticks.

The many species of mites have a variety of eating habits. Many mite species like really rotten stuff, and they feed on decaying plants and animals on the forest floor. Some mite species prefer to eat the fungi and bacteria that break down dead plants and fallen trees. As bark beetles and carpenter ants tunnel into fallen trees and the wood decays and becomes softer, mites move into fallen trees too. Most mites are about the size of the period at the end of this sentence. So you can see why they can eat only very small pieces of food.

One species of mite, the penknife mite, got its name because it can fold its head and legs inside its shell, just the way a pocketknife folds up. The mite folds up to protect itself from predators.

PENKNIFE MITE *(PTYCTIMIN)*, MAGNIFIED THOUSANDS OF TIMES ITS ACTUAL SIZE

some of it, leaving the rest as droppings. This process happens over and over again. The plant pieces get smaller each time, and a little bit more of them is digested each time.

Even among the small animals of the forest floor, there are predators. Centipedes are one of the larger arthropod predators. They move through the ground litter and the tunnels in fallen logs, hunting for the insects and slugs they eat. Centipedes have one pair of legs on each body segment, while millipedes have two pairs of legs on each segment. The centipedes in the old growth forest have claws, strong jaws, and venom glands to help them capture their prey. However, they are not poisonous to human beings.

Each millipede or mite takes only a very small bite out of the litter on the forest floor. How do they manage to chew up all the litter that falls to the ground in the old growth forest? They do it by sheer numbers. In just 10 square feet (1 square meter) of forest soil, there can be as many as 100,000 to 200,000 mites. You won't see them because they are so small. But they are underneath your feet. In fact, each time you take a step, your foot is being held up on the backs of about 16,000 invertebrates, which are standing on roughly 120,000 little legs.

CHAPTER 4
THE FOREST CANOPY

The many large branches of the big trees in the old growth forest provide a deep canopy. This multilayered canopy is a unique habitat that is not found in younger forests. So many plants and animals live in the old growth canopy that they form a unique community, separate in some ways from the rest of the forest below them.

From the ground, all you can see in the canopy is the branches swaying in the breeze. It looks very peaceful up there, high above the ground, sunny, and near the blue sky. Yet the canopy of the old growth forest is full of life, and it is an important part of the old growth forest's structure.

SO MANY PLANTS AND ANIMALS LIVE IN THE OLD GROWTH CANOPY THAT THEY FORM A UNIQUE COMMUNITY, SEPARATE IN SOME WAYS FROM THE REST OF THE FOREST BELOW THEM.

In some ways, the canopy is almost a small ecosystem of its own. The canopy has its own microclimate, which is the local climate of a small site. On a hot summer day, it is hot, sunny, dry, and breezy at the very top of the trees. Partway to the ground, in the middle of the branches, it is cooler, moister, and shadier. On the forest floor, it is comfortably cool and shady, except for patches of sunlight here and there. During a winter storm, the upper branches hold a lot of the snow. The canopy protects the forest floor from the snow, cold, and winds. It offers elk, deer, and other wildlife a sheltered place to stay until the storm is over.

Old growth Douglas firs develop some massive branches. These branches are somewhat flat on top and spread out almost like fan-shaped platforms near the tree trunk. They provide a lot of horizontal surface, and over time, a small amount of soil forms on top of them. Epiphytic plants—plants that grow on other plants—grow in this soil, forming gardens on the tree branches. Many epiphytes get their moisture and nutrients only from the air and rain. They are able to remove dissolved minerals from the water as raindrops flow over them. Other epiphytes depend partly on the soil perched on the large branches.

Epiphytic plants cover almost every surface of an old growth tree. More than one hundred species of mosses and lichens grow on old growth Douglas firs. The dry weight of the mosses and lichens on a single tree can be as much as 70 pounds (30 kilograms).

Lichens are actually double plants. The outer plant is a fungus. Inside the fungus, an alga grows. Since the alga needs a wet environment, it cannot live in open air. The fungus provides a protective covering, but allows sunlight to penetrate and reach the alga inside. The alga makes food from sunlight through photosynthesis, which the fungus cannot do. Together, the alga and the fungus are able to survive in all kinds of environments, even very harsh ones. Only certain combinations of algae and fungi form, and these combinations have been named as species.

ROOSEVELT ELK (CERVUS ELAPHUS) SHELTERING IN THE OLD GROWTH FOREST

A number of different kinds of lichens grow on old growth trees. Some lichens are gray or brown and look like crusty or scaly patches on the bark. Another group of lichen species are green and form hairy or branchy-looking tangled clumps that hang from branches. This group includes the common old man's beard lichen.

A third group of lichens are green and leafy looking. This group includes a lichen known as deer lettuce, which looks somewhat like leaf lettuce. Bright green on top, deer lettuce is white underneath. It is the dominant epiphytic lichen in old growth forests and is hardly ever found anywhere else. This lichen takes nitrogen from the air and makes it part of the plant. Deer lettuce is loosely attached to tree branches and breaks off during storms, falling to the ground in great quantities. When the fallen lichens decay, their nitrogen becomes available to other plants. Deer lettuce is an important source of nitrogen in the old growth forest.

(LEFT) **LICHENS ARE PLANTS THAT ARE PART FUNGUS AND PART ALGA.**
(ABOVE) **DEER LETTUCE *(LOBERIA OREGANA)* IS A TYPE OF LEAFY LICHEN.**

THE RED TREE VOLE (*Arborimus longicaudus*)

The red tree vole is a small rodent that lives high in the forest canopy. It is about 6 to 8 inches (15–20 centimeters) long and has brownish red fur above, with lighter-colored fur on its underside. Voles are about the size of mice but have small, round ears that are almost hidden in their fur. Red tree voles are active mainly at night.

A red tree vole may spend its entire life in a single old growth tree. Red tree voles build their nests on the large, flattened branches of old growth Douglas firs. Their favorite food is green Douglas fir needles, although they occasionally eat true fir and hemlock needles. They build their nests from twigs that they have stripped of needles.

Male and female tree voles have separate nests. Young voles leave their mother's nest when they are about one month old. In a large old growth Douglas fir, the young voles may move only to another branch on the tree to build their own nests. Generation after generation of tree voles may live in one giant tree, building nests up and down through all the branches, and out the length of the branches.

The nests have many chambers and tunnels with no special pattern. Tunnels may lead to the outside at various places in the nest. In addition to other exits, all vole nests have an escape tunnel that exits the underside of the nest near the tree trunk. The tree vole uses this tunnel to escape from predators such as raccoons, long-tailed weasels, and martens. Tree voles try to stay in their nests as much as possible, because spotted owls hunt for tree voles caught in the open on branches.

As a tree's lower branches die from lack of sunlight, the voles move higher, always staying near their food source, the green needles. The tree voles may live 150 feet (46 meters) or more above the ground. They stay in their homes through storms that make the treetop sway in the wind, waiting for the return of sunshine.

In the winter, deer and elk eat the deer lettuce that falls on top of the snow—that's how this lichen got its name.

Some animals make their homes in the forest canopy. You are unlikely to see them because they live high in the trees and they are often nocturnal, or active at night. A red tree vole may spend its entire life in the canopy, never once coming down to the ground.

The flying squirrel also nests in the canopy, in trees or large snags. This small squirrel is dark brown with very soft fur. It does not actually fly—it glides. The flying squirrel has a large, loose fold of skin along each side of its body, extending between its forelegs and hind legs. When the squirrel wants to "fly," it leaps from a high branch. It stretches its legs wide, spreading the loose folds of its skin like wings. Instead of falling, the squirrel glides down to the ground, steering with its forelegs and using its tail as a rudder.

Usually a flying squirrel glides to the ground to hunt for truffles, one of its favorite foods. The squirrels also eat lichens and nuts. While they are hunting for food, they must look out for predators that hunt

MARTEN (MARTES AMERICANA)

them, such as spotted owls or martens.

The marten is about two-thirds the size of a house cat. A member of the weasel family, it has a slender body with a long, bushy tail. It has a pointed snout with small ears. Its fur can vary from light to dark brown, and may even be an orange red color.

Like all weasels, martens are fierce hunters. They hunt for all kinds of squirrels, rabbits, voles, mice, and birds. Martens like to stalk along fallen trees or prowl through the treetops. In winter they follow snow tunnels along the sides of fallen logs. Martens are agile and fast and excellent tree climbers. Once they are in the canopy, they can run along the branches and jump from tree to tree, moving incredibly fast.

The canopy of the old growth forest supports hundreds of species of arthropods. Flies, gnats, butterflies, moths, and beetles can all be found in the canopy. Vaux's swift, a small, dark-colored bird, flies just above the canopy, darting after the many insects. The olive-sided flycatcher flies through and above the canopy, also hunting for insects.

Spiders are common at all levels of the forest. If you walk through the forest when the sun has just come out after a rainstorm, you will see spiderwebs everywhere. The webs are silvery and bright as the sunlight sparkles off the raindrops clinging to the webs. Long strands of spider webbing stretch from branch to branch, weaving the forest together in a silvery web.

CHAPTER 5
BIODIVERSITY AND CHANGE

The old growth forest has thousands of species of plants and animals—it is rich in biodiversity. Yet, only a few decades ago, foresters and scientists thought the old growth forest was a fairly simple ecosystem. They knew that because of its huge trees the old growth forest had a lot of biomass, possibly more than any other ecosystem on earth. But they thought the old growth forest was a "biological desert," an ecosystem with most of its living matter tied up in the wood of the big trees, and with only a few other plants and animals. After all, the quiet old growth forest didn't seem to have nearly as much life as nearby meadows and young forests, which were alive with birds flying and singing, flowers blooming, and butterflies visiting flowers.

It was only after scientists spent years doing research in the old growth forest that they began to discover its subtle diversity. It is rich in species of small mammals like voles and shrews, for example, instead of in large mammals like deer and bears. It is also home for many species of bats, including big brown bats, little brown bats, long-eared bats, and small-footed bats.

SMALL-FOOTED BAT (MYOTIS CILIOLABRUM)

Much of the old growth forest's biodiversity was harder to find and appreciate. The forest floor has thousands of species of arthropods, of insects and millipedes and mites. There is rich insect life in the tree canopy. From the top branch of the tallest tree to under the ground, the forest has many species of lichens and fungi, each one living in the particular habitat that best suits it.

Voles, bats, mites, lichens—it wasn't the kind of biodiversity that scientists started out looking for. But over the years, the more scientists have studied the old growth forest, the more biodiversity they have found. Although the ecosystem is built around just a few species of large, long-lived conifers, it is rich in all kinds of species. The old growth forest is much more than just lots of standing wood.

OVER THE YEARS, THE MORE SCIENTISTS HAVE STUDIED THE OLD GROWTH FOREST, THE MORE BIODIVERSITY THEY HAVE FOUND.

What difference does biodiversity make? You can't see all those bats and mites and lichens when you walk through the forest. Does it make any difference whether or not the forest has lots of different kinds of fungi, or would the forest get along fine with just a few different kinds?

HOW ECOSYSTEMS SURVIVE: DIVERSITY AND RESILIENCE

When an ecosystem has many species to carry out each function, that diversity gives resilience to the ecosystem. Resilience is the ability of an ecosystem to maintain its functions through environmental changes. The more biodiversity an ecosystem has, the more resilient it is. If only one species carried out a function, and this species was even temporarily wiped out by disease or wildfire, then the ecosystem would collapse. But a resilient ecosystem, like the old growth forest, has many species to carry out each function. It can survive many events, such as windstorms or outbreaks of disease or insects. A resilient ecosystem also recovers much faster from catastrophic events like wildfires or even volcanic eruptions.

The old growth forest's big trees, snags, fallen trees, and canopy create a rich variety of habitats. In turn, these many habitats make possible the diversity of species. The many different species, in their turn, carry on the functions of the ecosystem. A tiny penknife mite helps to recycle a huge fallen tree. A red-backed vole eating truffles carries spores to new places, spreading the mycorrhizal fungi that the big trees need. The deer lettuce on a tree branch takes nitrogen from the air and turns it into a solid substance. Then, when this lichen falls to the ground and decays, the nitrogen fertilizes the soil, helping to nourish other plants. Each species has a part to play in the ecosystem.

THE CHANGING FOREST

When you walk in an old growth forest, it's peaceful and quiet. It's easy to feel that the forest must have always been exactly like it is now, and that it will always be the same. But the old growth forest is constantly changing. A winter storm breaks the top off a tree, and it becomes a snag. A tree falls over, and young trees grow where it once stood, while the fallen tree slowly decays. Animals are born and grow up, and sometimes are captured by predators. These small, constant changes are part of the regular cycles of the old growth ecosystem. Energy and matter constantly flow through the ecosystem, as animals and plants carry out the ecosystem's various functions. These small, daily changes are the texture of life in the old growth forest.

Over the centuries, if it is undisturbed, the old growth forest undergoes a gradual transformation. Young Douglas firs cannot grow in the shade of older, established Douglas firs. Instead, western hemlocks, western red cedars, and true firs begin to grow in the shade of the forest canopy.

These trees grow well in shade, and eventually they dominate the lower levels of the forest. Gradually, as the large Douglas firs die and topple over, hemlocks, cedars, and true firs dominate the forest.

If an old growth forest is undisturbed by major changes for one thousand years, it becomes a climax forest, which is a different kind of ecosystem. Scientists used to think that the ecosystem's natural tendency was to reach a climax state, and then stay there. But as scientists studied forest ecosystems, they found that climax forests are rare.

Before Europeans arrived in the Pacific Northwest, the landscape was typically a mix of different kinds of ecosystems. Parts of the landscape were open prairies, with tall grass and scattered patches of forest. Other areas were young forest, some places were old growth forest, and a few areas were climax forest.

As scientists studied different ecosystems, they learned that large-scale changes, like forest fires or windstorms, are normal events. Although these dramatic events may happen only every few centuries in any one place, they are very important for shaping ecosystems. Large-scale change renews the forest.

The most typical large-scale events in the Pacific Northwest are forest fires, windstorms, landslides, forest diseases, and severe outbreaks of insects. Although volcanic eruptions are less common, the area does have some active volcanoes. The most recent major eruption was the 1980 eruption of Mount Saint Helens, in Washington State.

Most forest fires are started by lightning, so large fires are natural events. When a large fire has burned through a forest, the landscape is all black and gray. The once-green trees are snags, with their branches gone and their trunks charred black. The ground is covered with a thick layer of ash, all that's left of the plants and flowers of the forest floor. The forest looks completely destroyed.

But more is left of the forest than you see at first. Usually, most animals survive a forest fire. The large animals run. Smaller animals may find shelter inside or underneath fallen trees, which hold so

much moisture that they rarely burn completely. Fallen trees are also a source of nutrients and moisture for the plants that grow after the fire. Mycorrhizal fungi survive in the logs and underground. The seeds of trees and other plants often survive the fire too, hidden underneath the ashes, which contain nutrients that will help the seeds grow. Scientists call the snags, fallen trees, and seeds left from the old forest "biological legacies." The legacies are the gifts of the old forest to the new forest that will soon grow. With these gifts, the forest can recover.

The first summer after a forest fire, fireweed often covers much of the ground. The wind carries seeds from the cones of trees near the burned area. Douglas fir grows well on the open, bare ground left after a forest fire. Within a few years, many Douglas fir seedlings are growing across the burned area. They are the beginnings of a new forest. When the Douglas firs get taller, other species of trees begin to grow in their shade. Cavity-nesting birds and animals find homes in the snags left from the old forest.

Elk and deer come back to browse the grasses and young trees. Using the fallen trees for shelter, red-backed voles and other rodents eat truffles and distribute fungus spores back across the burned area.

A resilient ecosystem can recover faster after a forest fire or other event than a less diverse ecosystem can. Since a resilient ecosystem had many species before, it is likely to have enough species left after a fire to carry out all the functions of a healthy ecosystem. But even a resilient ecosystem needs time to recover from a forest fire. It takes time for trees to grow and for the new forest to develop a complex structure. It takes at least two hundred years for an old growth forest to develop again after a fire or other event has destroyed the old forest.

As a forest recovers and provides habitat, animals gradually return from neighboring forests that did not burn. Young animals travel to new areas when they grow up enough to leave their nest or first home. This process is called dispersal. The young animals must disperse to find their own home range, because the area

(ABOVE) **THE FIRST PLANTS TO RETURN AFTER A FIRE OR ERUPTION ARE ABLE TO GROW IN BARE GROUND AND OPEN SUN. THESE PLANTS ARE WHITE-FLOWERED PEARLY EVERLASTING** (*ANAPHALIS MARGARITACEA*), **YELLOW-FLOWERED DANDELIONS** (*TARAXACUM OFFICINALE*), **AND RED-FLOWERED FIREWEED** (*EPILOBIUM ANGUSTIFOLIUM*).

(TOP LEFT) **RECOVERY FROM A FOREST FIRE TAKES MANY YEARS. THE BIOLOGICAL LEGACIES OF THE OLD FOREST SUPPORT NEW LIFE IN THE RECOVERING FOREST.**

(BOTTOM LEFT) **LARGE MAMMALS SUCH AS THE BLACK-TAILED DEER** (*ODOCOILEUS HEMIONUS*) **OFTEN RETURN TO THE BURNED FOREST AS SOON AS THE NEXT YEAR, WHEN FRESH NEW GRASS GROWS IN THE BURNED AREAS.**

near the nest where they were born could not supply enough food for a constantly increasing population.

Birds can disperse over moderate distances, because they can fly. But many small animals disperse very slowly. The red tree vole, for instance, disperses only from tree to tree. The young voles normally will not travel across a wide area that has no large trees. The clouded salamander needs fallen trees to provide protection and moisture. It cannot cross an open, sunny area. It, too, moves back into the growing forest very slowly.

Like the red tree vole and the clouded salamander, many animals need connections between an existing old growth forest and the developing forest in order to move to the new forest. Fallen trees help to provide safe travel routes for small mammals, amphibians, and arthropods. Many of these animals need shade and moisture. The spotted owl needs the shelter of trees to protect it from its many predators. Some kinds of fungi and lichens also need a strip of connecting forest in order to travel to a developing forest.

CLOUDED SALAMANDER *(ANEIDES FERREUS)*

If a patch of developing forest becomes an island, without connections to other patches of forest, many species of animals and plants will never return to it. The isolated patch of forest will never regain all of its biodiversity. Eventually, it will become less resilient as an ecosystem, and less able to recover from outbreaks of insects or diseases.

A patch of forest that is cut off from other forests may lose species that it already has. All animals need a certain amount of habitat to survive as a species. The amount varies for each species, but it must be enough for a good-sized population of animals to feed, reproduce, and disperse. An isolated patch of forest may not have enough habitat to provide for all of its species, so some animals may not survive in small patches of forest. They can't find enough of the right kind of food, or they are eaten by predators, or they don't succeed in raising young. So an undisturbed old growth forest can lose biodiversity and gradually become a less resilient ecosystem.

CONNECTIONS BETWEEN EXISTING OLD GROWTH FOREST AND DEVELOPING FOREST ARE VITAL TO THE CONTINUATION OF THE ECOSYSTEM.

CHAPTER 6
PEOPLE AND THE OLD GROWTH FOREST

The first people to discover the old growth forests were Native Americans. Many Indian tribes have made their homes in the Pacific Northwest for thousands of years. The coastal Indian tribes, like the Haida and Makah tribes, built permanent villages near the ocean. They got much of their food from the ocean. Although the coastal Indians did some hunting in the forest, their main use of the forest was for wood.

The western red cedar was the most valuable tree to the coastal Indian tribes. They used logs for canoes and totem poles, wood for boards and roof shakes, bark for clothing and fishing nets, and roots for baskets. When the Indians needed wood, they took one tree at a time from the forest. They dropped trees and worked the wood by chopping with stone axes, or by using hot coals to burn through the wood.

The coastal Indians built longhouses out of heavy cedar planks, with cedar shake roofs. Longhouses kept out the heavy rains and the winds from ocean storms. Several

FOR MANY GENERATIONS, NATIVE AMERICANS IN THE PACIFIC NORTHWEST HAVE MADE TOTEM POLES FROM OLD GROWTH LOGS.

families from one clan lived in each longhouse. The Indians made cedar chests and other furniture for their longhouses. They also carved wooden masks that they used for religious ceremonies.

A totem pole stood in front of each longhouse, proudly showing what clan lived in that house. Each totem pole was carved from a single cedar tree. They often stood 50–70 feet (15–20 meters) high. One figure after another was carved into the tall pole—bear, raven, human, wolf, frog, and others—with creature stacked on top of creature. Each animal had specific meanings, and each totem pole told a story through the figures carved into it. The totem pole had religious and cultural meanings for the clan that owned it. The different figures often held personal meanings for the artist who carved the pole. The totem poles often lasted for seventy years or more, until they decayed and had to be replaced.

Many of the totem poles' stories have been lost. But perhaps we can understand a little bit about the importance a single tree had when it took on a new spiritual life as a totem pole. The Indian artists carved into the totem poles the richness of life that they saw around them. The animals stacked up on a totem pole echoed the richness of the old growth forest, where young trees grew out of fallen trees, ferns grew on tree branches, birds nested in snags, and animals lived in trees.

Many other Indian tribes lived throughout the Pacific Northwest, away from the coast. These Indians relied on fishing, hunting, and gathering plants for their food. Since they traveled more, moving with the seasons, these

THE ANIMALS STACKED UP ON A TOTEM POLE ECHOED THE RICHNESS OF THE OLD GROWTH FOREST, WHERE YOUNG TREES GREW OUT OF FALLEN TREES, FERNS GREW ON TREE BRANCHES, BIRDS NESTED IN SNAGS, AND ANIMALS LIVED IN TREES.

tribes did not build permanent wooden longhouses like the coastal Indians. The landscape of mixed younger and older forests provided a rich variety of foods for these Indians. They hunted deer and elk, which preferred areas where meadows were mixed with older forest. They gathered huckleberries and blackberries, which needed open, sunny places to grow.

Natural events helped to create the mix of meadows, young forests, and old growth forests. But since the Indians relied on the different areas for food, they took action to help create the varied landscape. In the fall, they set fires to burn the meadows. These fires burned off the dead grass and kept trees from growing. In the spring, the meadows were green with new grass. The Indians also set fires that burned through the forest. These fires helped to clear out the brush, which made it easier for the Indians to travel and to hunt deer and elk. The Indians set these fires late in the fall, and the fires usually did not burn hot enough to kill the larger trees. So for thousands of years, the Indians helped to shape the forests in the Pacific Northwest.

Europeans first explored along the coast of the Pacific Northwest in the 1700s. The first European settlers began to build houses and start farms in the early 1800s, along the lower Columbia River and the Willamette Valley. These pioneers saw the old growth forests as dark, gloomy, even frightening places. They wanted farms, and the trees were in their way. They also wanted lumber, and the trees were a source of wood. Very few pioneers saw the forests as places of beauty.

These early pioneers logged the easily reached forests along rivers and wide valleys first. They logged along the Columbia River, the Willamette Valley, the Oregon coast, and Puget Sound in Washington. The loggers used axes to cut the huge trees. Sometimes it took several men days to cut down a single big tree. They used teams of oxen to pull the logs out of the forest, and they floated the logs down the nearest river to a sawmill. By the late 1800s, logging and lumber were major industries in the Pacific Northwest. Ships came to Portland, Seattle, and other ports, and carried the lumber to San Francisco and the East Coast.

Logging continued to be a big industry in the Northwest through the 1900s. Over the years, steam engines replaced the oxen. Loggers built railroads into the mountains to haul out the logs. Eventually, the railroads were replaced by roads and logging trucks. The ax was replaced by the chainsaw, and modern logging equipment replaced the steam engines. The mills also added modern machinery for making boards and plywood out of logs.

Loggers have been cutting old growth trees in the Pacific Northwest for almost two centuries. Only small numbers of trees were logged at first. But after World War II ended in 1945, more trees were logged as millions of houses were built. Logging rates continued to grow as the population of the United States was growing. All those people needed houses, wood, and paper. Those products came from trees, many of them from old growth forests in the Pacific Northwest. Many logs were also shipped overseas, to other countries that needed wood.

After almost two centuries of logging in the Pacific Northwest, much of the original old growth forest has been logged. Most old growth on privately owned

THE OLD GROWTH FORESTS OF THE PACIFIC NORTHWEST HAVE BEEN LOGGED FOR NEARLY TWO HUNDRED YEARS. THIS PICTURE SHOWS OLD GROWTH (BACK LEFT), REGROWTH (BACK RIGHT), AND CLEAR-CUT FOREST (FRONT) SIDE BY SIDE.

timber lands has been logged. These lands are now covered with young forests, which are sometimes called tree farms. The millions of young trees growing in these tree farms will someday be logged in their turn, to provide more wood and paper for human use.

While these tree farms help meet an important need for wood, they cannot take the place of the old growth forests. They do not have the biological legacies of snags and fallen trees that are left after a forest fire. The young forests on tree farms do not have the complex structure of an old growth forest, so they cannot supply the diversity of habitats. The spotted owls, flying squirrels, and other animals of the old growth forest cannot survive in most tree farms.

If they were left untouched, it would take two centuries or more before these young forests could start to become old growth forests. But on a tree farm, the trees will probably be logged again in eighty years or even less, before they can develop into an old growth forest.

Most of the old growth forests that we have left are in the national forests and national parks. Three government agencies—the Forest Service, the National Park Service, and the Bureau of Land Management—manage these lands for the American people. Logging is allowed on some of the public lands, and so these lands have a mix of young forests, old growth forests, and other natural forests. The public lands are open to everybody, and many people enjoy hiking and camping in the forests.

Over the past two centuries, we have changed our ideas about old growth forests. The early pioneers wanted to get rid of the old growth forests. Over the years, we began to appreciate the beauty of the old growth forests. But we still thought they were biological deserts, without much life except big trees. Since the 1970s, we've begun to understand how unusual and special these forests are, and how rich they are in biodiversity. Think how much we might learn in the next decades, if the old growth forests are around long enough for us to keep learning.

THE FUTURE OF OLD GROWTH FORESTS

Many people have become more and more concerned about our remaining old growth forests. We now know that to preserve the old growth ecosystem, we must save more than scattered stands of big trees. To preserve all the species that are part of the old growth ecosystem, we must keep large areas of old growth forests. These forests must be close enough, with enough connections between them, for animals to travel between them. Even small animals, like clouded salamanders, must be able to travel from one area of forest to the next.

But how large should old growth forest preserves be? How much is enough? How close together do they need to be? How wide do the connecting forests between the preserves need to be? Scientists don't know all the answers yet.

There is much public debate about these questions. While old growth forests are important, people need wood and paper too. Also, many families in the Pacific Northwest depend on the jobs that logging and sawmills provide. Many people are concerned that we find a balance between preserving old growth forests and providing wood products and jobs.

Part of the answer may lie in how foresters manage forests where logging takes place. We've seen that forests can recover from catastrophic events like forest fires. Can forests recover in a similar way after logging? The answer is yes and no. Yes, they can—if the logging leaves behind biological legacies, such as snags and fallen trees, and if the forests are given enough

A MODERN LUMBER MILL IN MORTON, WASHINGTON

time. No, they can't—if everything is taken from the logged area, if careless logging leaves the soil bare so it washes away, if the forests aren't given enough time to recover, and if too large an area is logged.

The U.S. Forest Service, which manages national forests, is a leader in developing better ways to log that do less damage to the ecosystem. With these new methods, loggers leave snags, some green trees, and some logs. The logged area is replanted with several species of trees, not just Douglas fir. The result is a young forest that is more like a natural forest than a tree farm. Since this young forest has more structure, it provides more habitats for a wider variety of species. When managed forests provide more habitats, animals that need these habitats have more places to live than just in the old growth forests. It's also easier for animals to travel between the remaining patches of old growth forest.

Of course, it's very important what happens to the old growth forests themselves. An important question is how foresters should take care of the old

growth preserves. One scientist, Dr. Daniel Botkin, says that nature preserves are not like strawberry preserves. He means that you can't take old growth forests, put them in a jar on a shelf, and expect them to stay just the way they are. Old growth forests are constantly changing in small and large ways. If the forests are protected from large-scale changes, like forest fires, they eventually become a different kind of forest. How much natural change, like forest fires and insect outbreaks, should we allow to take place in old growth forests? Should we replace natural fires with controlled fires?

There is much public debate over these questions. Many scientists, however, fear that if we wait too long to make decisions, some species that need old growth forests will go extinct. Some of these species are already threatened or endangered, which means that they are in danger of becoming completely extinct. The spotted owl is the most famous threatened species, but there are others.

Does it make a difference if a species becomes extinct? After all, most of us will never get to see a spotted owl anyway. Some scientists have compared our situation to that of people sitting in an airplane. Imagine you are sitting in an airplane, waiting for it to take off. Then imagine that you see somebody outside the plane popping rivets out of the plane. The plane has thousands of rivets, and it can fly if it's missing just one rivet, or even a few dozen rivets. It's hard to say just how many rivets would have to be missing before the plane would come apart in the air and crash. But when you're going to fly in that plane, you don't want any rivets to be missing. You don't want to find out how many rivets the plane could lose and still fly.

Some scientists say that ecosystems are like airplanes and their rivets. An ecosystem can continue without one species. It can continue even if it's missing a few species. But sooner or later, if the ecosystem keeps losing species, it will collapse. It makes a lot of sense, then, to try to make sure that no more species go extinct.

THE PACIFIC YEW

Biodiversity is important for a healthy ecosystem. But does it matter to people? Yes, it does. People value old growth forests for a variety of reasons, and so it's important that these forests continue to be healthy ecosystems. But it also makes a difference to people that individual species continue to survive.

The story of one species, the Pacific yew tree, shows why biodiversity is

BARK OF A PACIFIC YEW TREE *(TAXUS BREVIFOLIA)*

important to people. The Pacific yew grows in the shade underneath old growth trees. Next to the huge, magnificent trees of the old growth forest, the yew tree looks small and ugly. It usually grows to only 20 to 30 feet (6 to 9 meters) tall, and the champion yew tree is only 54 feet (16 meters) tall. Often the Pacific yew has several trunks, giving it a shrubby look, and the trunks are often crooked. The thin, reddish bark peels away from the trunk, making the tree look ragged and half-dead.

Although the orange red yew wood is hard, strong, and durable, it is often crooked and the small trees do not provide very much wood. In the past, it was sometimes used for bows and fence posts, but often it was simply ignored. When loggers cut other trees, they left the yew trees behind. Often, they were burned after the logging was done. The Pacific yew was thought to be of little value.

A few years ago, however, scientists found that yew trees contain taxol, a chemical that is valuable in treating cancer. When they first discovered taxol, scientists were unable to make the chemical in their laboratories. The only source was the yew tree. Suddenly, there was a great demand for yew bark, which was the best source of the new drug. It took a lot of yew bark to produce just a small amount of taxol, so there was a demand to harvest thousands of yew trees. From being tossed aside as useless, yew trees had suddenly become the most valuable trees in the forest.

Taxol made from yew bark was used to treat thousands of cancer patients. So many yew trees were harvested that many people became concerned that we would cut too many trees and destroy the species. Foresters set up yew reserves and took other steps to make sure this did not happen. Scientists have learned how to make taxol in their laboratories, and the demand for yew bark has dropped. But if it hadn't been for the small yew tree, living in the shade of the big old growth trees, this valuable cancer drug would never have been discovered. Scientists think that there may be many other valuable discoveries in the old growth forest, perhaps in some ordinary fungus or insect that now seems to have no value at all.

GIFFORD PINCHOT NATIONAL FOREST, WASHINGTON

WHAT YOU CAN DO

What can you do to help old growth forests survive? Here are some ideas.

Be careful about how many wood products you use. If we would all use fewer wood products, and recycle paper and cardboard, then fewer trees could be cut. The old growth forests could be left alone and our need for wood and paper could be satisfied by logging from other forests. Reuse cardboard boxes and paper bags several times if you can. Try not to waste paper, cardboard, or wood. Recycle as much cardboard, paper, and newspaper as you can. Sometimes wood can be reused or recycled too.

Visit old growth forests if you can. If you live in the Pacific Northwest or your family is going there for a vacation, contact any national forest or national park to find out where their old growth forests are. You'll find some addresses at the end of this book. You can also find national forests and parks in the phone book under listings for the federal government. The

National Park Service is listed under the Department of the Interior. The U.S. Forest Service is an agency of the Department of Agriculture.

Most national parks and forests in the Pacific Northwest have hiking trails through old growth forests. The old growth forest is a beautiful, peaceful place for hiking, and you'll have fun seeing for yourself some of the things you've read about in this book. When you visit the old growth forest, you show that people care about old growth forests.

Most old growth forests are on national lands. The U.S. government decides how national lands are managed. In recent years, Congress has considered a number of different laws about the old growth forests. Some of the proposed laws would protect most of the old growth forest, while other laws would protect smaller amounts, leaving some old growth forest open for logging.

Now that you have learned about the

old growth forest, you may want to express your views. Watch newspapers and magazines for articles about proposed laws that would affect old growth forests. Then find out all you can about the proposed law. Once you have decided what you think about the proposal, write a letter to your senator or representative. These officials listen to what people say about laws proposed to protect the old growth forests. These national lands are public lands, and the public has a voice in what happens to them.

Here are some addresses you can use to express your views on how the old growth forests should be managed on publicly owned lands.

To write to the president:

The President
The White House
Washington, D.C. 20500

To write to the senators from your state:

The Honorable (name of your senator)
United States Senate
Washington, D.C. 20510

To write to your representative in Congress:

The Honorable (name of your representative)
U.S. House of Representatives
Washington, D.C. 20515

WEBSITES TO VISIT FOR MORE INFORMATION

Many government agencies and nonprofit groups have websites with more information about the old growth forests of the Pacific Northwest. Just a few of these websites are listed below.

American Forests

<http://www.americanforests.org/>

American Forests is the nation's oldest nonprofit citizens' conservation organization. Their website contains information about programs such as Global ReLeaf, which helps people improve the environment by planting and caring for trees, as well as resources such as the National Register of Big Trees.

Forest Conservation Portal

<http://forests.org/>

Forests.org, Inc. is a nonprofit group that works to end deforestation, preserve old growth forests, and conserve other forests. The site contains a wide variety of forest conservation links, including both recent and archived news articles.

Tidepool

<http://www.tidepool.org>

Tidepool is a project by the nonprofit group Ecotrust. The nonprofit Tidepool news service collects stories from dozens of online news sources. Subjects include forests and other environmental subjects. Their site is updated five days a week with the latest news.

National Forests of Oregon and Washington

<http://www.fs.fed.us/r6/r6nf.htm>

This site, published by the Pacific Northwest Region of the U.S. Forest Service, provides information on the national forests in the Pacific Northwest.

Pacific Northwest Research Station

<http://www.fs.fed.us/pnw>

The U.S. Forest Service, Pacific Northwest Research Station, is an excellent source of science information on all types of forests. The site offers links to science publications and web pages where teams of scientists report their newest results.

FOR FURTHER READING

Behler, Deborah A. *The Rain Forests of the Pacific Northwest.* New York: Benchmark Books, 2001.

Hickman, Pamela. *In the Woods.* Halifax, Nova Scotia: Formac Publishing Company Ltd., 1998.

Kittinger, Jo S. *Dead Log Alive!* New York: Franklin Watts, 1996.

Lauber, Patricia. *Volcano: The Eruption and Healing of Mount St. Helens.* New York: Bradbury Press, 1986.

Leuzzi, Linda. *Life Connections: Pioneers in Ecology.* New York: Franklin Watts, 2000.

McClung, Robert M. *Lost Wild America: The Story of Our Extinct and Vanishing Wildlife.* Hamden, CT: Linnet Books, 1993.

Pandell, Karen. *Journey through the Northern Rainforest.* New York: Dutton Children's Books, 1999.

Patent, Dorothy Hinshaw. *Biodiversity.* New York: Clarion Books, 1996.

Russo, Monica. *The Tree Almanac: A Year-Round Activity Guide.* New York: Sterling Publishing Company, 1993.

Scott, Michael. *Ecology.* New York: Oxford University Press, 1995.

Staub, Frank. *America's Forests.* Minneapolis, MN: Carolrhoda Books, Inc., 1999.

VanCleave, Janice. *Ecology for Every Kid: Easy Activities That Make Learning about Science Fun.* New York: John Wiley & Sons, 1996.

Walker, Sally M. *Water Up, Water Down: The Hydrologic Cycle.* Minneapolis: Carolrhoda Books, Inc., 1992.

Whitman, Sylvia. *This Land Is Your Land: The American Conservation Movement.* Minneapolis: Lerner Publications Company, 1994.

NATIONAL PARKS AND NATIONAL FORESTS WITH OLD GROWTH DOUGLAS FIR FORESTS

CALIFORNIA

Klamath National Forest
1312 Fairlane Road
Yreka, CA 96097

Six Rivers National Forest
507 "F" Street
Eureka, CA 95501

OREGON

Crater Lake National Park
P.O. Box 7
Crater Lake, OR 97604

Mt. Hood National Forest
16400 Champion Way
Sandy, OR 97055

Rogue River National Forest
333 W. 8th Street
P.O. Box 520
Medford, OR 97501

Siskiyou National Forest
P.O. Box 440
Grants Pass, OR 97526

Siuslaw National Forest
P.O. Box 1148
Corvallis, OR 97339

Umpqua National Forest
P.O. Box 1008
Roseburg, OR 97470

Willamette National Forest
P.O. Box 10607
Eugene, OR 97440

WASHINGTON

Gifford Pinchot National Forest
6926 E. 4th Plain Blvd.
P.O. Box 8944
Vancouver, WA 98668

Mt. Baker-Snoqualmie National Forest
Skykomish Ranger Station
74920 NE Stevens Pass Hwy.
P.O. Box 305
Skykomish, WA 98288

Mt. Rainier National Park
Star Route, Tahoma Woods
Ashford, WA 98304

North Cascades National Park
2105 Highway 20
Sedro-Woolley, WA 98284

Olympic National Forest
1835 Black Lake Blvd. SW
Olympia, WA 98512

Olympic National Park
600 East Park Avenue
Port Angeles, WA 98362

GLOSSARY

arthropods: animals that have a segmented body, jointed legs, and a hard casing on the outside of their bodies instead of bones; some examples are insects, spiders, and centipedes

biodiversity: the number of different species of plants and animals living in an ecosystem

biomass: the total weight of all living plants and animals in a given area

canopy: the horizontal upper layer of the forest formed by the tree branches

cavity: a hole in a snag or live tree

cavity-nesting animals: animals that live in holes in snags or live trees

composition: the different species of plants, animals, fungi, and bacteria that live in an ecosystem

conifer(s): a tree that has needles and produces its seeds in cones; most conifers are evergreen. Some common conifers are pines, firs, spruces, hemlocks, and cedars.

coniferous forest: a forest in which most of the trees are conifers

deciduous trees: trees that lose their leaves in the fall and grow new leaves in the spring

decomposers: organisms that break down plant and animal matter into simple nutrients that can be used again by plants

dispersal: the process in which young animals leave the nests in which they were born to find their own home range

dominant species: the species of plant or animal that is the most common in an ecosystem, or the species that has the most influence on the ecosystem

ecosystem: a community of plants and animals, along with their nonliving environment

endangered: in danger of becoming extinct

epiphytic plants: plants that grow on other plants

functions: processes that go on in an ecosystem. Functions include birth, growth, reproduction, death, and decay.

habitat: the place where a plant or an animal normally lives and grows

hardwoods: trees that have leaves and produce their seeds in flowers; most hardwoods are deciduous. Some common hardwoods are maple, oak, beech, and hickory.

invertebrates: animals without backbones

larvae: insects in an early stage of their development

lichen: a "double plant" consisting of an alga growing inside a fungus

litter: the natural debris, including needles, leaves, and twigs, that falls to the forest floor

microclimate: the local climate of a small site, which may vary from the area's general climate

mycorrhizal fungi: fungi that grow on plants' root tips and help the roots to absorb water and nutrients from the soil

nocturnal: active at night

nurse log: a fallen tree that has rotted enough for young trees to grow on top of it

photosynthesis: the process by which green plants use sunlight, carbon dioxide, and water to make their own food

resilience: the ability of an ecosystem to maintain its functions through environmental changes

saprophytic plants: plants that get all or part of their energy from decaying plant or animal matter, instead of from photosynthesis

snag: a standing dead tree

structures: the physical parts of an ecosystem, such as rocks and logs

taxol: a chemical found in the Pacific yew tree that is valuable in treating cancer

threatened: likely to become endangered in the future

truffles: underground fruiting bodies of mycorrhizal fungi

INDEX

ABOUT THE AUTHOR

Valerie Rapp is a science writer. She is the winner of a 1996 fellowship in nonfiction from Literary Arts, Inc., in Oregon. Ms. Rapp has worked in natural resource management since 1978. In addition to writing scientific and technical publications about forests, rivers, and watersheds, she has had jobs in wildland firefighting, trail work, timber sale planning, and wild and scenic river planning.

She has a B.A. in English literature from the University of Buffalo, New York. She lives with her husband, Gene Skrine, in Portland, Oregon. Three stepchildren are also an important part of her family.

Her book, *What the River Reveals: Understanding and Restoring Healthy Watersheds*, explains how we've changed our rivers in the Pacific Northwest and what we can do to restore our rivers and watersheds. She is also the author of *Life in a River* in Lerner's Ecosystems in Action series.

In all her writing, she focuses on the complex relationships between people and nature.

PHOTO ACKNOWLEDGEMENTS

Additional photographs are reproduced with the permission of: © Joe McDonald/CORBIS, p. 13 (left); © Gary Braasch/CORBIS, p. 23; David Meardon/U.S. Fish and Wildlife Service, p. 24 (top); © Rick & Nora Bowers/Visuals Unlimited, p. 24 (bottom); Oregon Department of Fish and Wildlife, p. 26; © Jim Yuskavitch, pp. 29 (both), 51 (bottom), 52, © David Evans Walter, p. 38; Oregon Natural Resources Council, p. 43; © Rob Simpson/Visuals Unlimited, p. 46.